Curriculum Visions Explo

Exploring the first civilisations

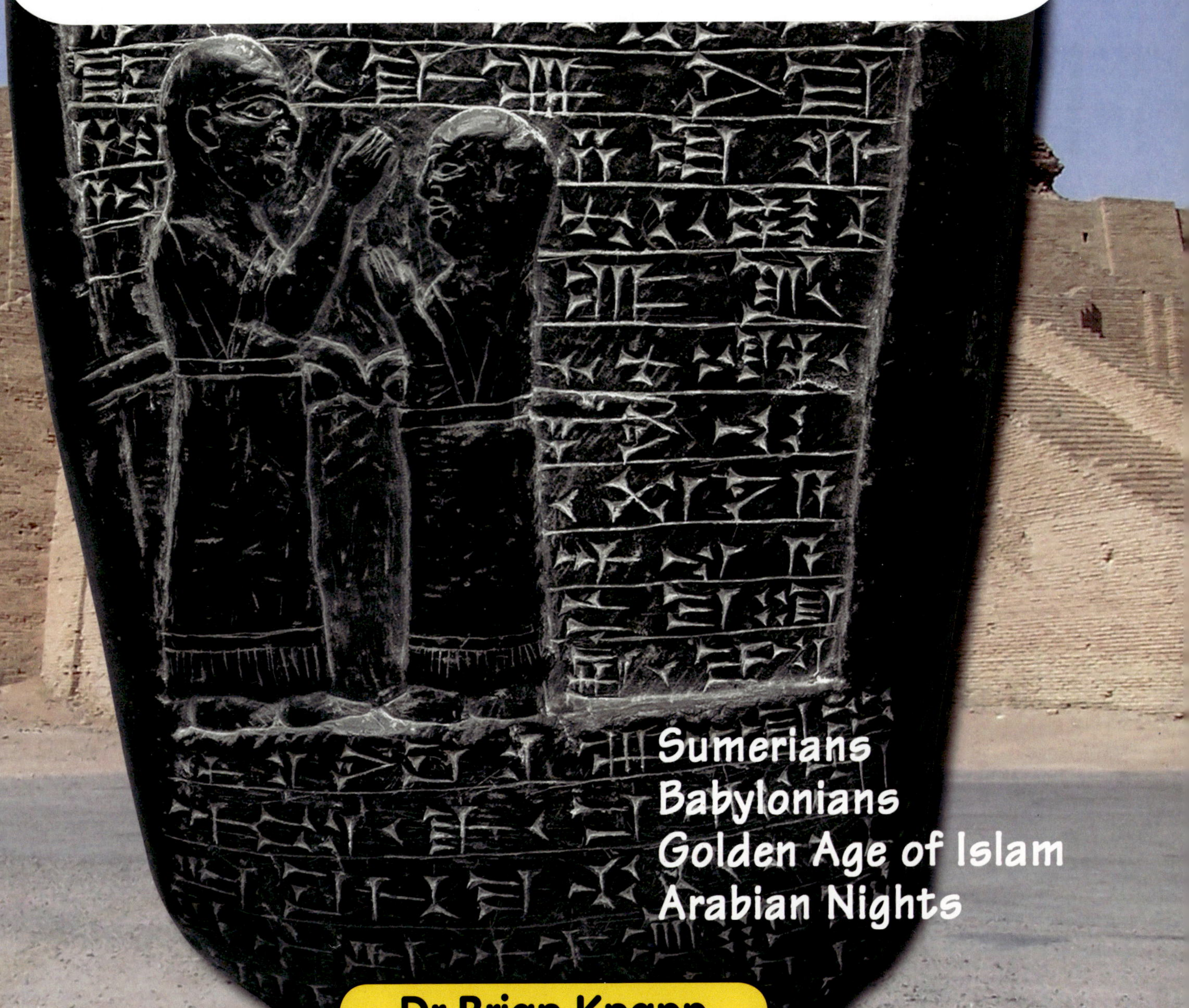

Sumerians
Babylonians
Golden Age of Islam
Arabian Nights

Dr Brian Knapp

World history

First Middle East civilisations (11000BC–1268AD)

| 11000 BC | 10000 BC | 9000 BC | 8000 BC | 7000 BC | 6000 BC | 5000 BC |

Middle East timeline

First permanent villages in the area of Mesopotamia

People grow crops in the Fertile Crescent

| 11000 BC | 10000 BC | 9000 BC | 8000 BC | 7000 BC | 6000 BC | 5000 BC |

Ancient Egyptians (3000–332BC)　　　　　　　　Second World War (1939–1945)

4000 BC　3000 BC　2000 BC　1000 BC　0　1000 AD　2000 AD

Ancient Greeks (800–146BC)　Anglo-Saxons (450–1066)　Vikings (800–1066/1400)　Tudors (1485–1603)　Victorians (1837–1901)

Romans (700BC–476AD)

Contents

Where civilisation began 4
Meet the people of Mesopotamia 6
The first farmers 8
The first machines 10
The dawn of writing 12
The mighty city of Ur 14
Ziggurat temples 16
Amazing art 18
The Middle East at war 20
Babylon 22
The Golden Age of Islam 26
The Arabian Nights 28
Glossary and index 32

Look up the **bold** words in the glossary on page 32 of this book.

The Sumerians build towns and start to use writing
Fortress city of Erbil is founded
The Sumerians build the Ziggurat of Ur
The city of Babylon is founded
The Assyrians attack the Sumerians and capture Ur
Persian ruler Darius captures Babylon and other cities
Empires and cities in Mesopotamia become less powerful
Ur is abandoned
Mongol ruler from Asia, Genghis Khan, captures and destroys Baghdad

4000 BC　3000 BC　2000 BC　1000 BC　0　1000 AD　2000 AD

The Sumerians build the city of Ur
The Hanging Gardens of Babylon may have been built
Ancient Greek ruler Alexander the Great captures Babylon
Alexander the Great dies. Babylon destroyed
Arab rulers build a new city – it comes to be known as Baghdad
Golden Age of Islam Many science books and the Arabian Nights are written in Baghdad

Baghdad

The land of the first civilisations is called Mesopotamia. It included world-famous cities like Babylon.

Egypt and the Pyramids of North Africa.

Q Where is the Middle East?

Where civilisation began

This is a book about some of the first people to write and to live in cities. People who do both of these things are called 'civilised'. They are very different to people who wander about gathering food.

These people lived in the Middle East, just inside Asia and close to Africa. Their part of the Middle East was called Mesopotamia.

This region has dry, hot summers, so much of it is **desert**. But there are also two big rivers. Forests once grew by the banks of these rivers and wild animals roamed among them. So, at first, early peoples had lots to eat – but only if they lived close to the rivers.

But as the numbers of people grew, they started to run out of food. Finding out how to get more food was to change the way they lived.

Did you know… ?

- In **Stone Age** times, most people lived in widely scattered small **tribes**.
- Most people wandered over the countryside gathering nuts, fruit and roots and hunting wild animals.
- The people who lived in the deserts of the Middle East had to live by rivers, so they could not wander about.
- The people of Mesopotamia became civilised before the Egyptians.

Meet the people of Mesopotamia

The word Mesopotamia was made up by the ancient Greeks, who once ruled there. But the Greeks were not the first people to make this part of their **empire**. They were simply one of a whole line of people who controlled this area.

Mesopotamia was the land where we now find the modern country of Iraq. The capital of Iraq is Baghdad, and Baghdad has an important part to play in our history. But it is quite a recent city compared to the cities that went before. So to find out about this area we have to go back over ten thousand years.

The Middle East is a place of deserts and rivers. It is hard for people to make a living in the desert, but near to rivers they have water and **fertile** land. This is why, right from early times, they were forced to live quite close together.

The land by the rivers was highly prized and in short supply, and so kings fought over it. That is why we shall see that one empire replaced another over the centuries. You had to be a strong king to keep control, and when a strong king died and was replaced by a weak one, there were always strong neighbours ready to take over and make their empire bigger.

Did you know…?

- The main rivers of this area are the Euphrates and the Tigris.
- The people who made the world's first empire were called the Sumerians. They invented the world's first writing and lived in the world's first city. Nearby were other people – the Assyrians. They often fought to control the area. But there were others, too, such as the Babylonians.
- Most of the people of Mesopotamia fought with ancient Egypt for control of the Middle East.

This map shows some of the famous places you will read about. The world's first city – Ur – is near the bottom. Babylon is further north. Right at the top is another capital city called Nineveh. Baghdad is in the centre. The whole area around the rivers Euphrates and Tigris is known as Mesopotamia.

7

The first farmers

Many thousands of years ago people began to see if they could make more of the land. They became the world's first farmers.

They tried growing different kinds of wild grass, keeping back the ones that grew best, and planting their seeds the next year. They did this year after year until what had once been small seeds of wild grasses were fat seeds of wheat.

The farmers also took wild animals and, in time, made them tame (domesticated).

The Middle East was ideal for those early farmers because there was warm weather for much of the year, and water in the rivers. It became such a wealthy area it was known as the 'fertile crescent'.

Did you know… ?

- The first people would have found plenty of fish in the rivers and wild animals to hunt, such as the bull and the boar.
- Wheat, barley, flax, chick pea and lentil were first grown here.
- Cows, pigs and sheep were all developed here.
- In the Stone Age, these farmers used animal horns tied to wooden branches to dig up soil and plant seeds. It was the world's first farming tool, and is called an adze.
- The **Bronze Age** farmers replaced the animal horn with a metal blade. This is still used all over the Middle East even today.

Q What crops did they plant?

They ground wheat seeds to make flour using two stones.

The first machines

Getting water out of the rivers and into the fields was a hard task in the dry season because the river level falls so far below the banks. So the farmers had to learn how to get water from the rivers to their fields.

They invented a way of using buckets on swivelling poles (shadoufs) as well as a system of buckets on wheels (Persian wheels) to raise the water out of the rivers.

In this way people in the Middle East had invented the first crops and the first way to water them and give a bigger crop.

 **What was a Persian wheel for?**

Did you know… ?

- The River Euphrates flooded every year. The flood waters could cover wide areas of land next to the river. This allowed seed to grow. But to keep it growing the soil had to be watered.
- The shadouf worked like a lever. The bucket of water was balanced by a heavy stone on the other end. It was a simple machine. But it needed men to work it.
- The Persian wheel turned a wheel on a shaft. The shaft could be turned using animals. This was the first time anyone had used animals for powering machines.

The dawn of writing

One of the earliest known ways of writing was invented six thousand years ago. The letters were made by pressing the cut end of a piece of stiff grass (a reed) into a sheet of wet clay. The clay was then left to harden. The writing was then literally 'set in stone'.

They only had one little triangle shape to work with, so they made little pictures with it. You can see some of them below.

They made many of these little clay tablets with all kinds of information on, and, incredibly, two million still survive.

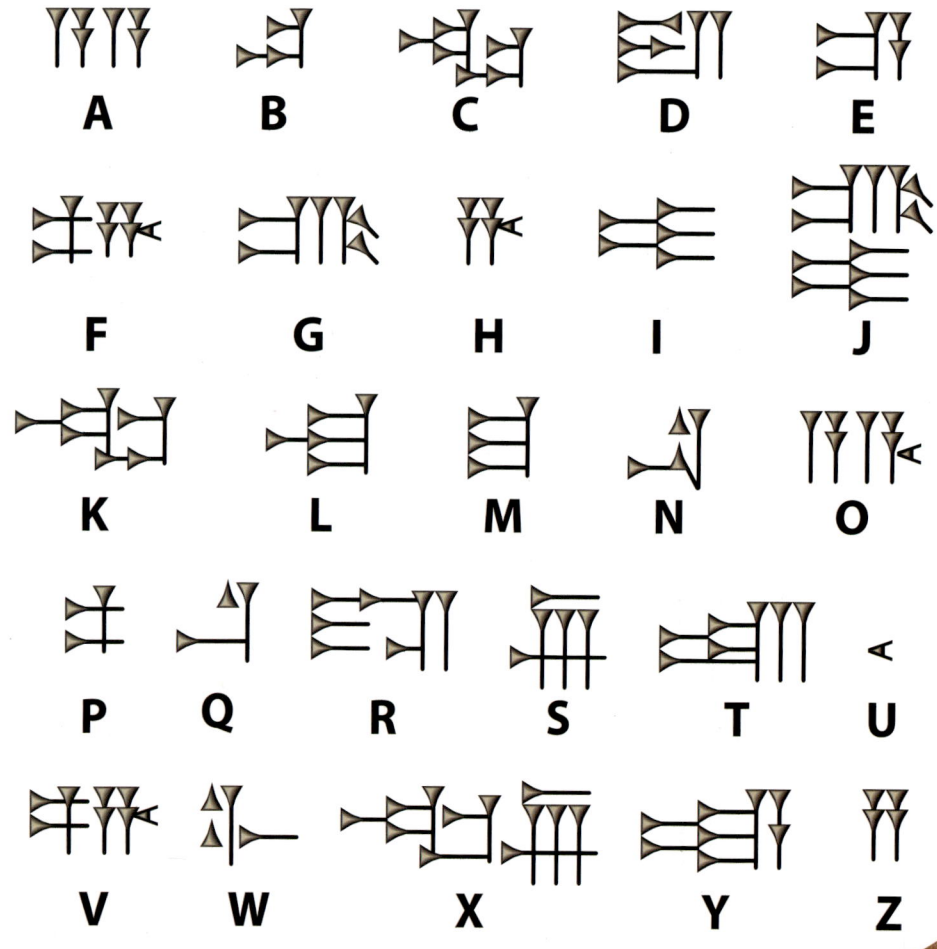

Did you know… ?

- The writing is known as 'cuneiform', which means 'wedge-shaped'.
- Cylinder seals were invented about the same time as writing.
- Cylinder seals were so important that they were placed in **tombs** of powerful people when they died.
- Most seals have a hole through their centres, so they may have been worn as part of a necklace. That way no one else could use the owner's seal, and the seal was always to hand when needed.

What the writing looked like pressed into brown clay and cut into black stone.

The first signatures

Nowadays we might put a seal on a document in wax. A seal is a kind of signature pressed into something. The people in the city of Ur invented signatures.

The signatures that they invented were little pictures cut into a stone cylinder. That is why they are called cylinder seals. It was something like a wine cork in size and shape, but made of stone.

The cylinder was rolled over a piece of clay, making a mark on the clay which was the same as the picture that had been cut into the seal.

13

Did you know…?

- The first city had 65,000 people in it.
- The buildings were nearly all made out of sun-baked mud. They made thatched roofs using reeds from the riverbanks.
- The city was surrounded by a mud wall.
- Ur is now far from the river and the sea. That is because the Euphrates has changed its course. **Silt** brought by the river over the centuries also built out the land into the sea.

Here you can see the remains of one of the world's oldest cities. Notice the buildings were made with mud bricks. The Ziggurat of Ur is the building in the background.

The mighty city of Ur

Over the centuries, the farmers of Mesopotamia learned how to grow more food than they needed. This meant some people could become full-time **craftsmen**, priests and so on. That is why, about six thousand years ago, the first towns in the world grew up. The craftsmen exchanged the goods they made for the food the farmers had over. The craftsmen became very skilled and made the beautiful things you can see in this book. It was a **revolution**.

That is how the world's first city – called Ur – grew up. It was founded about 5,800 years ago and lasted for 3,000 years before being abandoned.

The first people who lived there were called Sumerians. They chose a spot where they could have crops and water nearby and so they could begin trading. That is why they built Ur beside the River Euphrates and close to the sea.

The city was named after the local god, Nanna. Ur means "the place where Nanna lives". People believed, just like other ancient peoples, that gods lived on Earth as well as in heaven, and needed an earthly home of their own as close to heaven as possible. This is why the people built a great temple to their god, which stretched up towards the heavens. We call this tall, step-like temple a ziggurat. The Ziggurat of Ur is one of the most famous early buildings in the world.

Q What did people in Ur do?

Ziggurat temples

The people in the Middle East were ruled by kings with great power. They made everyone spend some of their year building great monuments. In nearby Egypt they built **pyramids** (picture on the right) made of stone blocks. The pyramids were tombs for **pharaohs**.

The Sumerians, Babylonians and others thought differently. They built giant temples to their gods, not their kings. They built the temples as steps, one step upon another. They used bricks. On the top step they built a **shrine** to their gods.

Pyramid in Egypt under construction.

Did you know… ?

- The Ziggurat of Ur is 64m long and 46m wide. It may originally have been over 30m tall.
- People got to the top of a ziggurat by walking up long ramps made of steps.
- Some ziggurats had a spiral ramp from bottom to top. It made the ziggurat look like a helter skelter.
- The people thought the ziggurats were the earthly home of their gods.
- The original bricks had coloured glaze surfaces that must have shone in the sunshine.

Q What was a ziggurat used for?

The ziggurats were much taller than this. The upper parts disappeared long ago. The lower walls of this ziggurat have been rebuilt recently.

Amazing art

These early Middle Eastern peoples were fine artists, and the works they have left behind are of high quality.

The peoples of Mesopotamia mainly sculpted things in clay and stone, or made mosaics using coloured stones. They did not make paintings, although they did paint their **sculptures**.

The Sumerians, the people who lived in the city of Ur, sculpted people with large, staring eyes, and showed men with long beards.

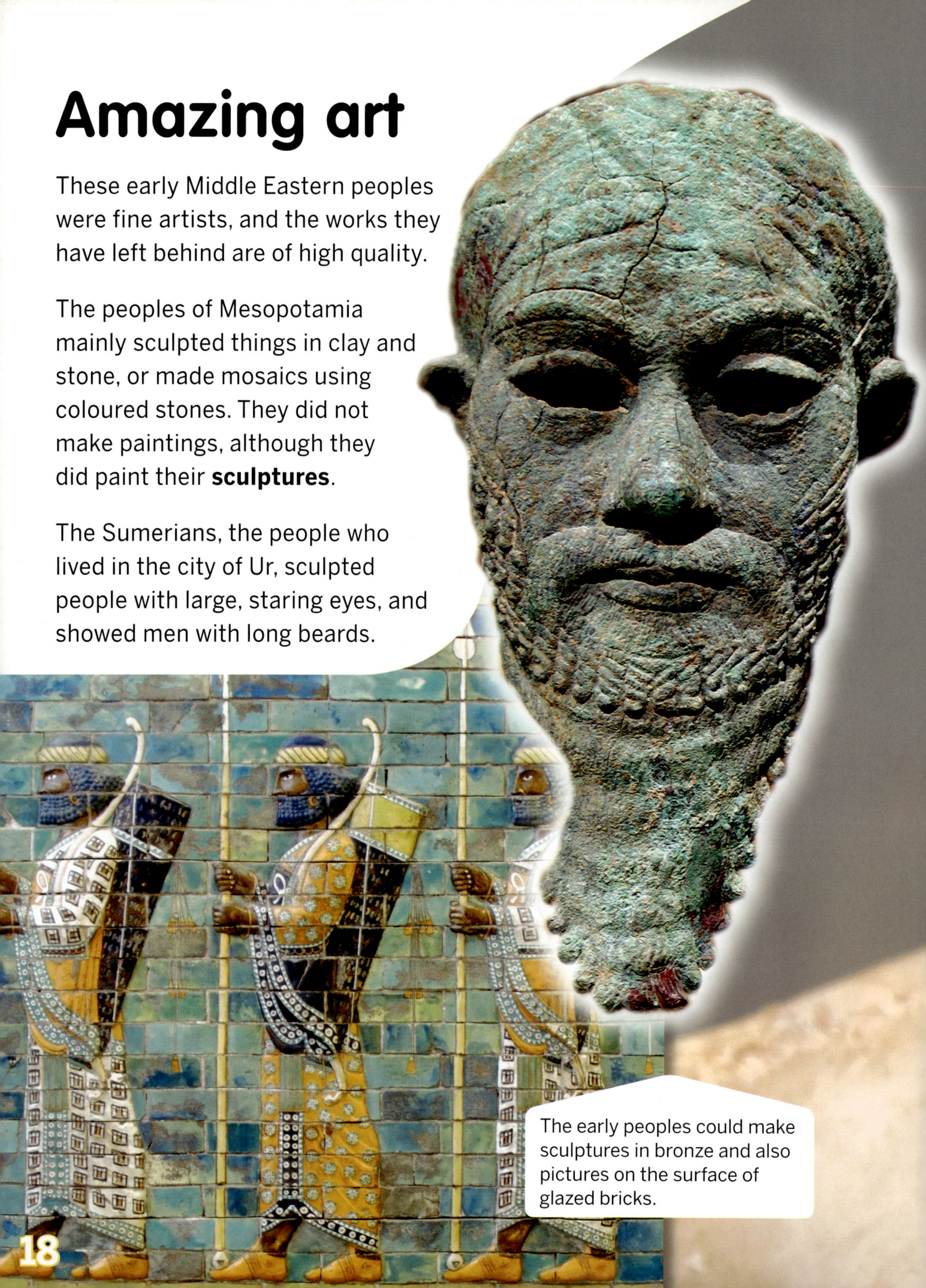

The early peoples could make sculptures in bronze and also pictures on the surface of glazed bricks.

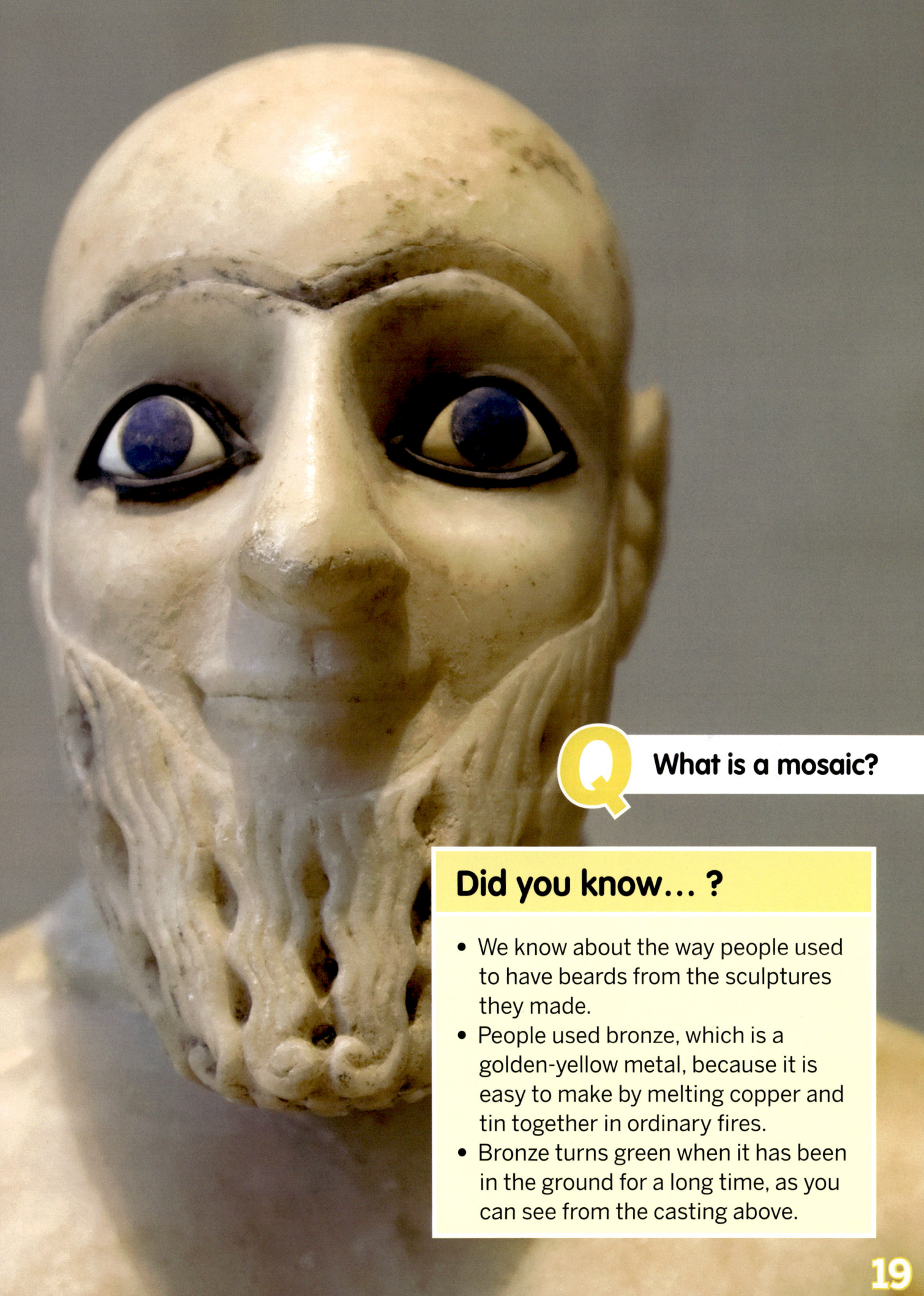

Q What is a mosaic?

Did you know… ?

- We know about the way people used to have beards from the sculptures they made.
- People used bronze, which is a golden-yellow metal, because it is easy to make by melting copper and tin together in ordinary fires.
- Bronze turns green when it has been in the ground for a long time, as you can see from the casting above.

The Middle East at war

In this rich region there were many powerful cities. Each city tried to become more powerful than its neighbour. As a result, cities were often at war.

Many of the artworks we see today show details of these wars. This is what helps us to understand how the people fought and what they used as weapons.

On this page you can see that they used bows and arrows, axes and swords. Some soldiers were foot soldiers (infantry) and others used chariots pulled by animals (cavalry).

Did you know…?

- The king of Ur is shown as the largest person in the middle of the top row because he was the most important person, not because he was the biggest person.
- They had solid wheels to their carts and chariots because spoked wheels had not been invented.
- They showed defeated people as being trampled underfoot.
- They used donkeys for their chariots because horses were unknown in the ancient Middle East.

This fabulous wooden box is called the 'Standard of Ur'. The pictures of Ur at war are made with tiny pieces of shell and coloured stones and held together by a kind of tar. It is about four and a half thousand years old.

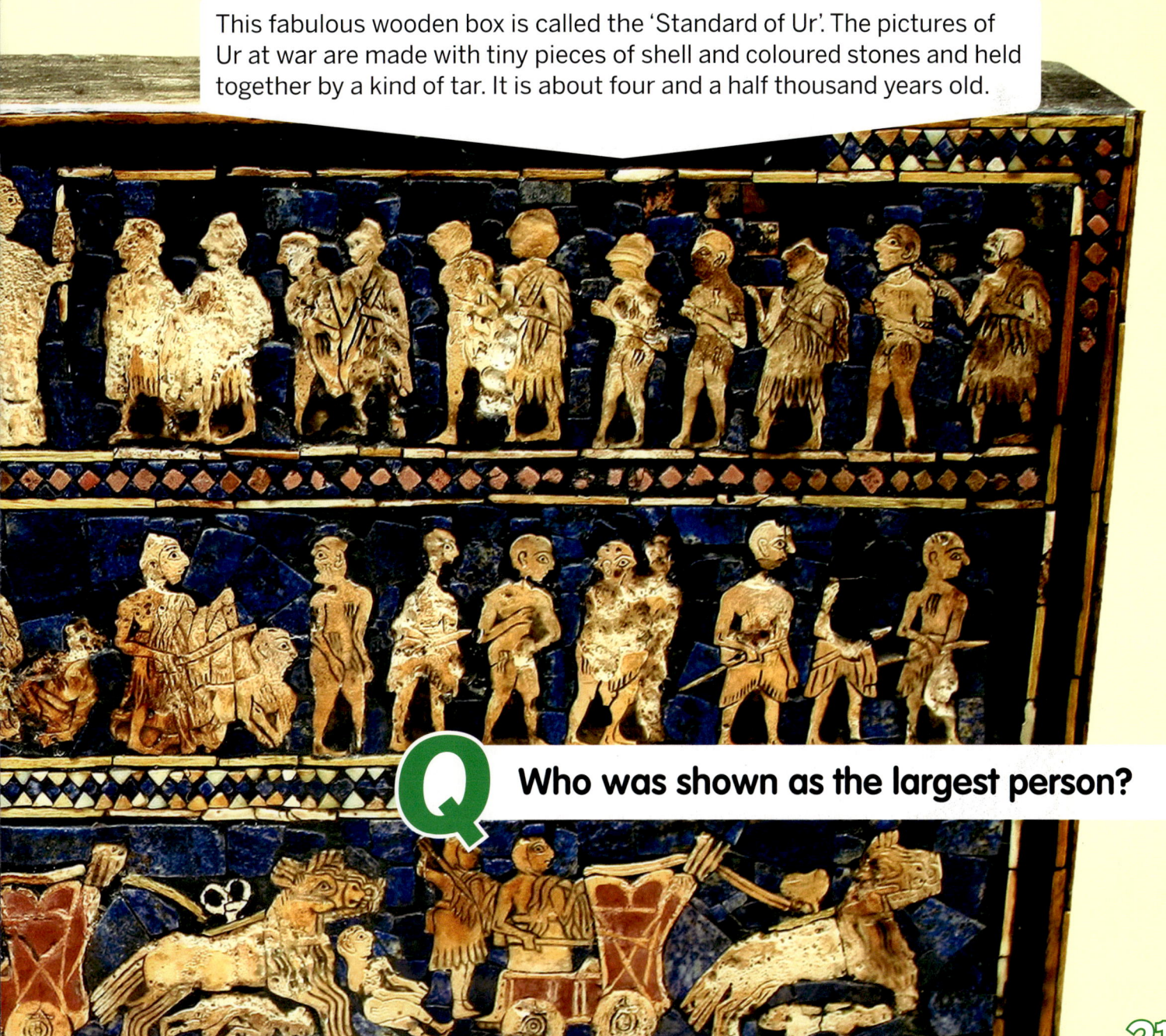

Q Who was shown as the largest person?

Did you know... ?

- The Seven Wonders of the Ancient World were: the Hanging Gardens of Babylon, Iraq; the Great Pyramids of Giza, Egypt; the Temple of Artemis at Ephesus, Turkey; the Statue of Zeus at Olympia, Greece; the Mausoleum (tomb monument) at Halicarnassus, Turkey; the Colossus (a giant statue) of Rhodes, Greece; and the Lighthouse of Alexandria, Egypt.
- Of the Seven Wonders of the Ancient World, only the Great Pyramids of Giza still stand today.

Babylon today. Part of the wall has been rebuilt to show what it was like many centuries ago.

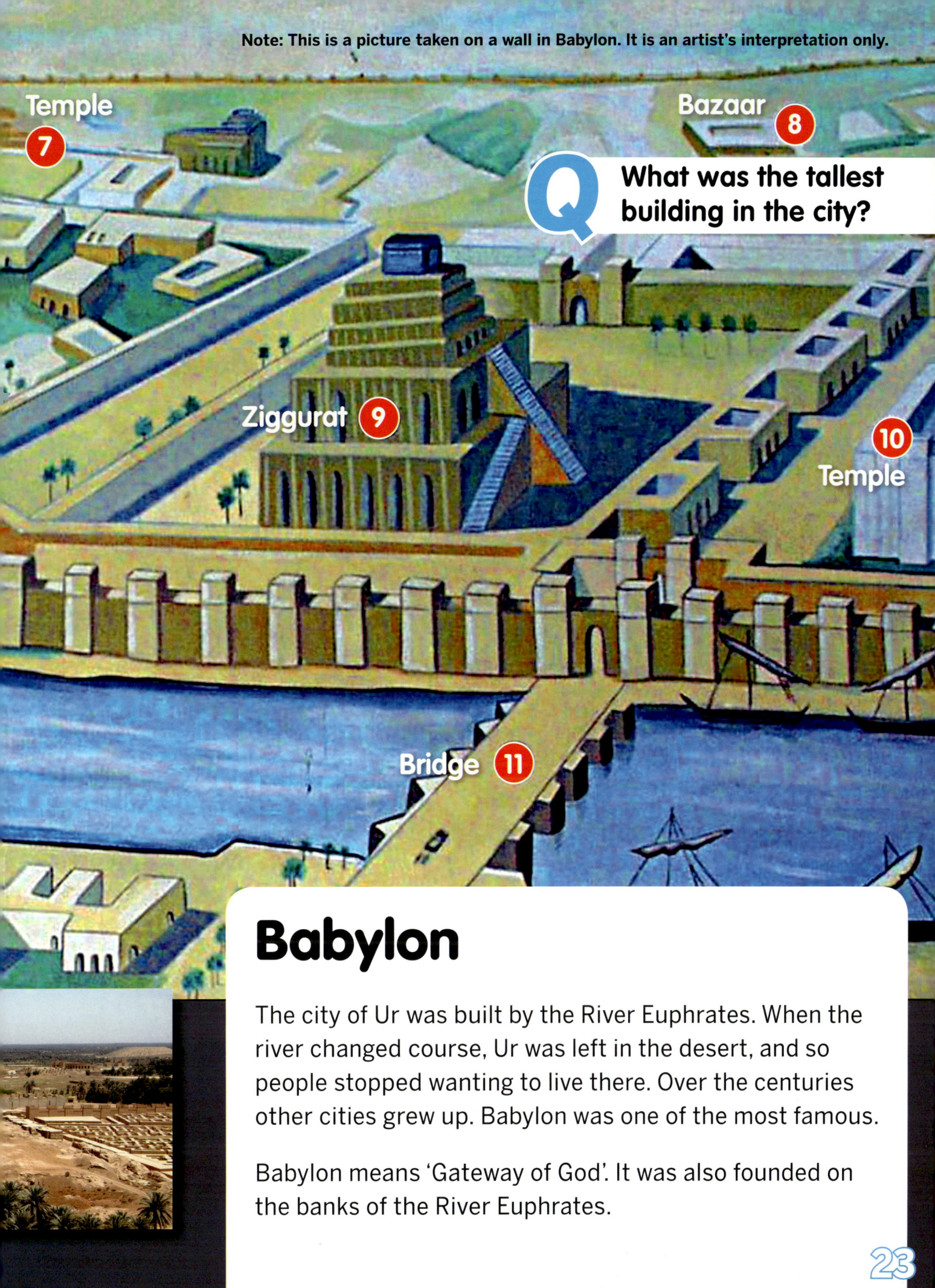

Note: This is a picture taken on a wall in Babylon. It is an artist's interpretation only.

Temple 7
Bazaar 8

Q What was the tallest building in the city?

Ziggurat 9
Temple 10
Bridge 11

Babylon

The city of Ur was built by the River Euphrates. When the river changed course, Ur was left in the desert, and so people stopped wanting to live there. Over the centuries other cities grew up. Babylon was one of the most famous.

Babylon means 'Gateway of God'. It was also founded on the banks of the River Euphrates.

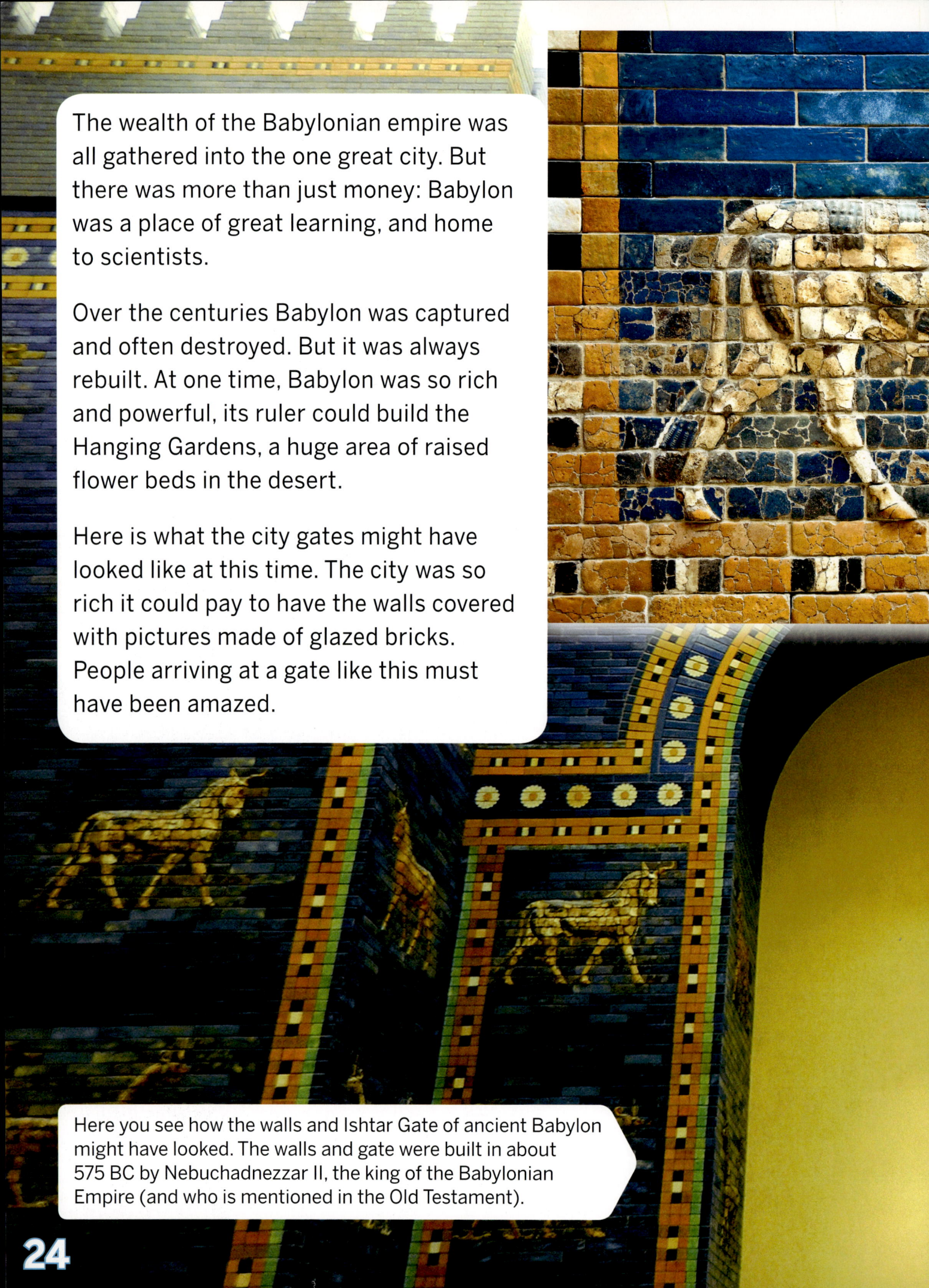

The wealth of the Babylonian empire was all gathered into the one great city. But there was more than just money: Babylon was a place of great learning, and home to scientists.

Over the centuries Babylon was captured and often destroyed. But it was always rebuilt. At one time, Babylon was so rich and powerful, its ruler could build the Hanging Gardens, a huge area of raised flower beds in the desert.

Here is what the city gates might have looked like at this time. The city was so rich it could pay to have the walls covered with pictures made of glazed bricks. People arriving at a gate like this must have been amazed.

Here you see how the walls and Ishtar Gate of ancient Babylon might have looked. The walls and gate were built in about 575 BC by Nebuchadnezzar II, the king of the Babylonian Empire (and who is mentioned in the Old Testament).

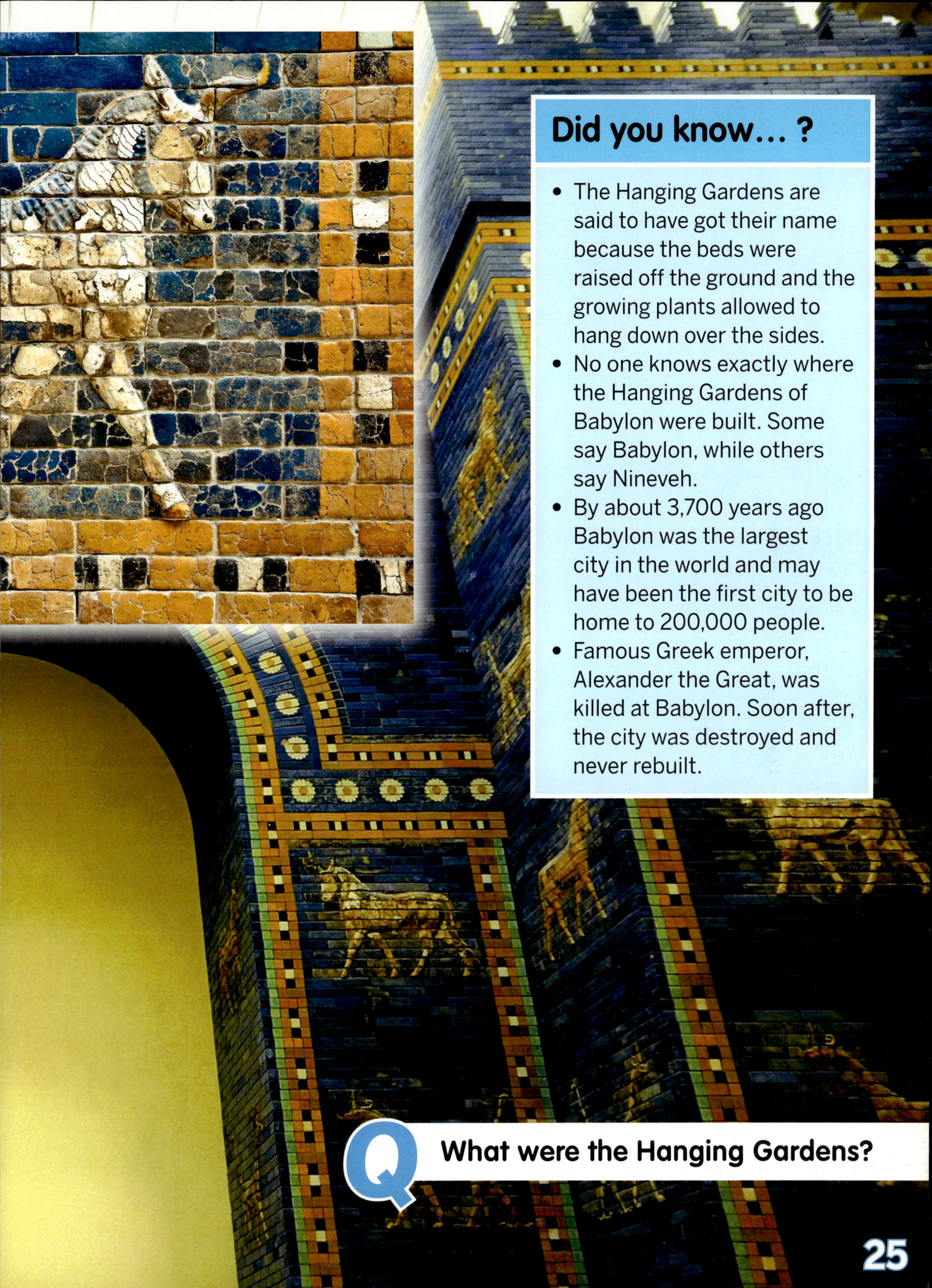

Did you know…?

- The Hanging Gardens are said to have got their name because the beds were raised off the ground and the growing plants allowed to hang down over the sides.
- No one knows exactly where the Hanging Gardens of Babylon were built. Some say Babylon, while others say Nineveh.
- By about 3,700 years ago Babylon was the largest city in the world and may have been the first city to be home to 200,000 people.
- Famous Greek emperor, Alexander the Great, was killed at Babylon. Soon after, the city was destroyed and never rebuilt.

Q What were the Hanging Gardens?

25

The Golden Age of Islam

Fifteen centuries ago, the Prophet Muhammad founded Islam using the truths given to him by Allah.

From then on, the Islamic faith spread through the Middle East. The time between the 8th and 13th centuries is called the Golden Age of Islam, and its centre was to be just north of the ruins of Babylon – a place called Baghdad.

Baghdad was built on the banks of the River Tigris. Baghdad was a planned city. It was built in the 8th century when a powerful local ruler decided to build a new capital city. This place would be called Baghdad.

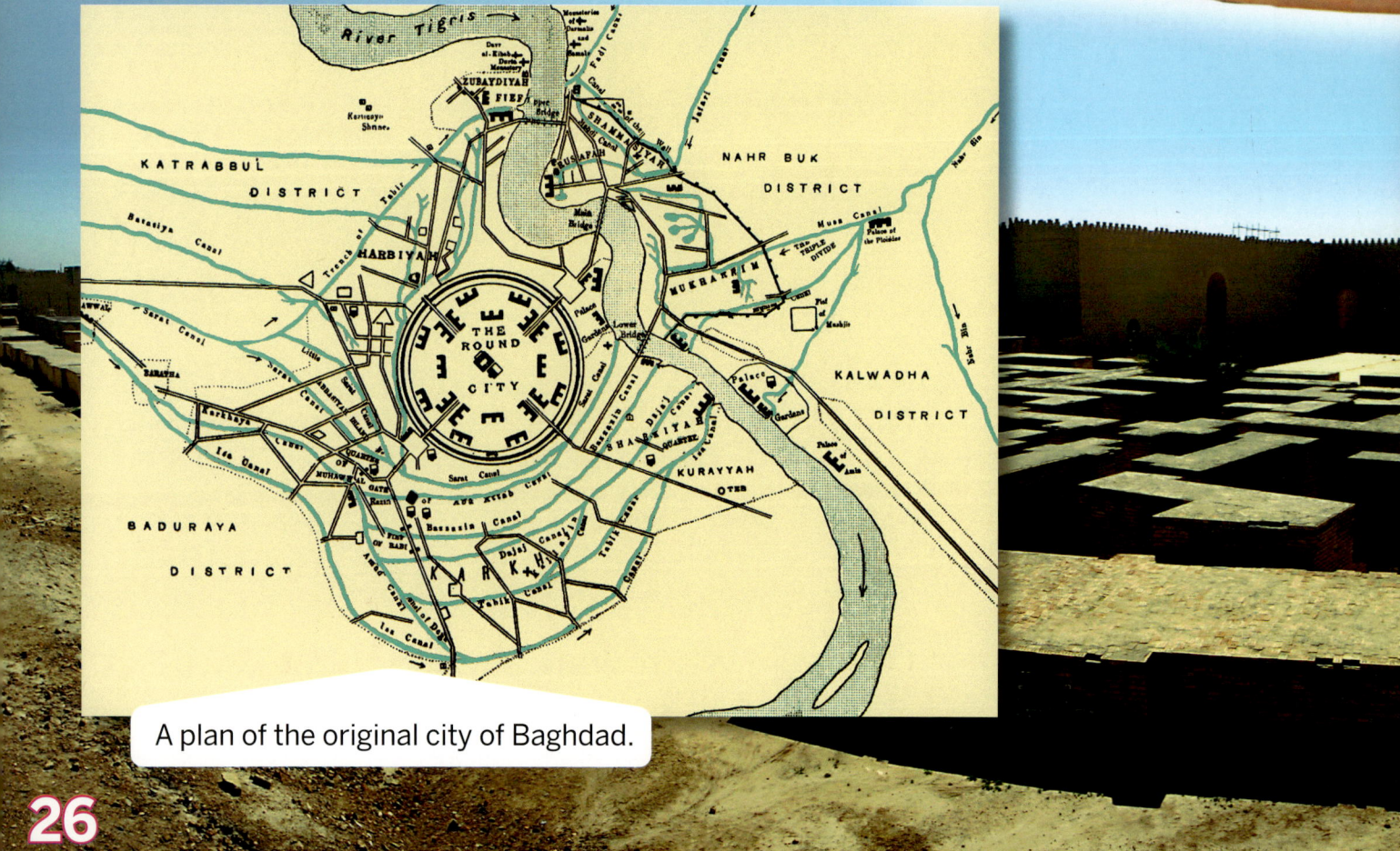

A plan of the original city of Baghdad.

An original manuscript from the Golden Age of Islam.

Did you know… ?

- On the outside was a city wall surrounded by a **moat**.
- Because it was a royal city, it had very wide streets.
- In the centre there was a new mosque, not a temple as there had been in old cities.
- The ruler decided to build a new House of Wisdom – a university. From then on, the people of Baghdad led the world in science, thinking, medicine and education.
- In the House of Wisdom all the ancient books and papers from Greece, Rome, and other parts of the world were translated into Arabic, so that all the knowledge was all in one place, in one language.
- In 1206, Genghis Khan became a powerful leader of the Mongol people of central Asia. He captured and destroyed Baghdad in 1258. The Golden Age of Islam was over.

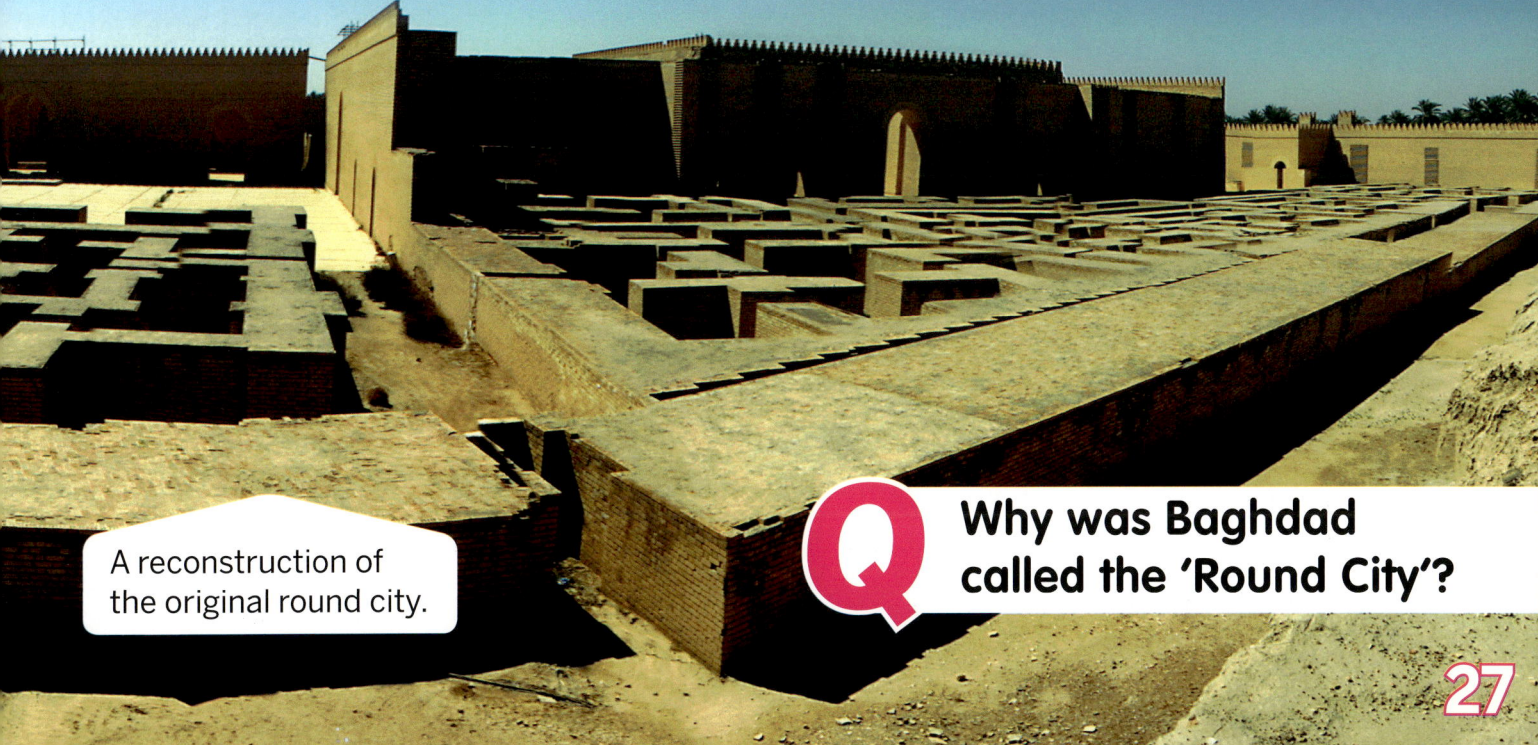

A reconstruction of the original round city.

Q Why was Baghdad called the 'Round City'?

The Arabian Nights

Many great works of science were gathered together in Baghdad during the Golden Age of Islam. But the scholars were also interested in gathering all of the folk tales that they could find from around the world. This is how the *One Thousand and One Nights (The Arabian Nights)* came to be written.

They were famous because of the way they were all fitted together as though they were one long story, when actually they came from far and wide.

Each story begins in the same way. A Persian king (Shahryar) marries a new bride (he had many wives). But then he discovers that his brother's wife is unfaithful. He also finds out that his own wife is unfaithful and has her executed. He is very upset by his wife's unfaithfulness and decides that all women are the same. So he begins to marry a line of women, only to execute each one the morning after the marriage, before she has a chance to be unfaithful. Eventually the vizier, whose duty it is to provide

Did you know…?

- The first earlier versions of *The Arabian Nights* have fewer than 1,001 stories.
- Many of the famous stories, such as 'Ali Baba and the 40 thieves', and 'Sinbad the Sailor', were not part of the original *Arabian Nights*, but were added in recent centuries.
- *The Arabian Nights*, like so much of Islamic writing from the Golden Age of Islam, came to us when medieval monks in southern Spain (which used to be part of Islam), began to translate the ancient books that the Muslims had left behind.
- The story of 'Ali Baba and the 40 thieves is where you find the famous phrase "Open, sesame!". Ali Baba uses it to open a cave.

The original book.

the women, cannot find any more. Scheherazade, the vizier's daughter, offers herself as the next bride, and her father eventually agrees.

On the night of their marriage, Scheherazade begins to tell the king a tale, but does not end it. The king, curious about how the story ends, cannot execute her because he needs to hear the end of the story. The next night, as soon as she finishes the tale, she begins, but does not finish, a new one, and the king puts off her execution again. So it goes on for 1,001 nights.

On the next page you will find an example of a story that is thought to be one of the original tales.

 **Why were the stories told?**

The fisherman and the genie

There was an old, poor fisherman who cast his net four times a day. One day he went to the shore and cast his net. When he tried to pull it up, he found that it was heavy. When he dived in and pulled up the net, he found a dead donkey in it. Then he cast his net again and pulled up a jug full of dirt. Then he cast his net for a third time and pulled up pieces of pottery and glass. On his fourth and final try, he called upon the name of God and cast his net. When he pulled it up he found a copper oil lamp with a cap that had the seal of Hebrew King Solomon on it.

The fisherman was overjoyed, since he could sell the oil lamp for money. But he was curious to know what was inside the oil lamp, and took off the cap with his knife. A plume of smoke came out of the oil lamp, and in its place stood a genie. The fisherman was frightened, although at first the genie did not notice him. In fact, the genie thought that Solomon had come to kill him. When the fisherman told him that Solomon had been dead for many centuries, the genie was very happy and granted the fisherman a choice of the manner of his death. That was not quite what the fisherman had in mind.

The genie said that for the first hundred years of being locked in the oil lamp, he swore to make the person who freed him wealthy beyond his dreams. But nobody freed him. For the second century, he swore to grant the one who freed him great wealth, but nobody freed him. After another century, he swore to grant three wishes to the person who freed him, yet nobody did so. After four hundred years of imprisonment, the genie became angry, and swore to grant the person who freed him only a choice of deaths.

The fisherman pleaded for his life, but the genie would not change his mind. So the fisherman decided to trick the genie. He asked the genie how he managed to fit into the oil lamp. The genie, eager to show off, shrank and placed himself back into the oil lamp to show how clever he was. The fisherman quickly put the cap back on, and threatened to throw it back into the sea. The genie pleaded with the fisherman, and swore to help him in return for being released. The fisherman accepted, and released the genie. The genie then led the fisherman to a pond with many fish, and the fisherman caught four. Before disappearing, the genie told the fisherman to give the fish to the Sultan. The fisherman did so, and was rewarded with money.

Every time a fish was fried on the first side, a person would appear and question the fish, and the fish would give an answer. But when the fish was flipped in the pan, it would be burnt and could not be eaten.

The Sultan asked the fisherman where he got the fish, and went to the pond to uncover their mystery. When he reached the pond, the Sultan found a Prince who was half stone and half man. After the Prince had told the story of how this came about, the Sultan helped him to get out of the stone and seek revenge on the person who had put him there.

The Sultan and the Prince became close friends. As a reward for the fisherman, the Sultan chose the fisherman's son to be his treasurer, and the Sultan and the Prince married the fisherman's two beautiful daughters.

The end

Glossary

Bronze Age
The time after the Stone Age, when people learned to use bronze.

craftsmen
People who are skilled at making things, for example, pots or swords.

desert
A place where it hardly ever rains and where very few plants can grow.

empire
A large area of many peoples all ruled by one king or emperor.

fertile
Soil that will allow crops to grow well.

moat
A ditch around a walled home or city designed to help keep attackers away. A moat is often filled with water.

pharaoh
A popular name for a king of Ancient Egypt.

pyramid
A shape with four sides that rises from a square base with the sides coming together at a point.

revolution
A change that affects everything.

sculptures
Carvings that can be seen in the round.

shrine
A place where people worship their gods.

silt
Very fine soil material carried by rivers during floods.

Stone Age
A very long period of time when people used stone and other natural materials because they have not invented metal.

tomb
A burial chamber above the ground.

tribe
A group of people who are often related.

Index

Arabian Nights/Thousand and One Nights 28-29, 30-31
art 18-19, 20-21
Bronze Age 8, 32
city 14-15, 20, 23, 24, 25, 26-27
civilisation 4
craftsmen 15, 32
desert 5, 6, 23, 32
empire 6, 24, 32
farming 8-9, 10, 15
fertile 6, 8, 32
Fertile Crescent 8
gods 15, 16-17
Hanging Gardens of Babylon 22, 24-25
Islam, Golden Age of 26-27, 28-29
king/ruler 6, 16, 21
knowledge 24, 26-27
machines 10-11
pharaoh 16, 32
pyramid 16, 22, 32
revolution 15, 32
river 5, 6, 7, 8, 10, 23
sculpture 18-19, 32
seal, cylinder 12-13
Seven Wonders of the Ancient World 22
shrine 16, 32
silt 14, 32
Stone Age 5, 8, 32
temple 15, 16-17
tomb 13, 16, 32
tribe 5, 32
war 6, 7, 20-21
writing 7, 12-13
ziggurat 14, 15, 16-17, 22-23

Curriculum Visions

Curriculum Visions Explorers
This series provides straightforward introductions to key worlds and ideas.

You might also be interested in
Our other ancient civilisations books such as The Stone Age, Celtic Times, The ancient Egyptians, The ancient Greeks, The Romans in Britain and Ancient Rome.

www.CurriculumVisions.com
(Subscription required)

© Atlantic Europe Publishing 2014

The right of Brian Knapp to be identified as the author of this work has been asserted by him in accordance with the Copyright, Designs and Patents Act 1988.

All rights reserved. No part of this publication may be reproduced, stored in a retrieval system, or transmitted in any form or by any means, electronic, mechanical, photocopying, recording or otherwise, without prior permission of the copyright holder.

Author
Brian Knapp, BSc, PhD
Senior Designer
Adele Humphries, BA, PGCE
Editors
Gillian Gatehouse
Emily Pulsford, BA
Designed and produced by
Atlantic Europe Publishing
Printed in China by
WKT Company Ltd

Exploring the first civilisations – Curriculum Visions
A CIP record for this book is available from the British Library.
Paperback ISBN 978 1 78278 077 9

Picture credits
All photographs are from the Earthscape and ShutterStock Picture Libraries, except 22: Wikipedia.

This product is manufactured from sustainable managed forests. For every tree cut down at least one more is planted.